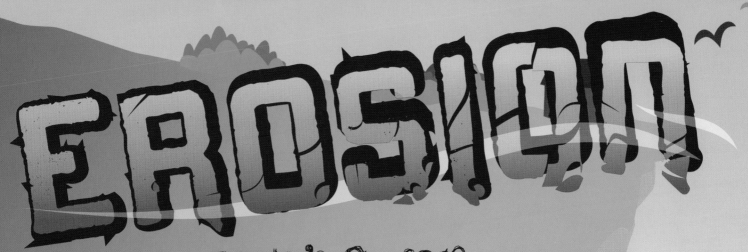

EROSION

Changing Earth's Surface

by Robin Koontz

illustrated by Matthew Harrad

PICTURE WINDOW BOOKS
Minneapolis, Minnesota

Thanks to our advisers for their expertise, research,
and advice:

Jeffrey R. Pribyl, Ph.D.
Professor of Chemistry and Geology
Minnesota State University, Mankato

Susan Kesselring, M.A., Literacy Educator
Rosemount-Apple Valley-Eagan (Minnesota) School District

_____

Editors: Jacqueline Wolfe and Nick Healy
Designers: Ben White and Brandie E. Shoemaker
Creative Director: Keith Griffin
Editorial Director: Carol Jones
The illustrations in this book were created digitally.

This book was produced for Picture Window Books by
Bender Richardson White, U.K.

Picture Window Books
1710 Roe Crest Drive
North Mankato, MN 56003-0669
877-845-8392
www.capstonepub.com

Library of Congress Cataloging-in-Publication Data
Koontz, Robin Michal.
Erosion : changing Earth's surface / by Robin Koontz ;
illustrated by Matthew Harrad.
p. cm. — (Amazing science)
ISBN-13: 978-1-4048-2195-8 (hardcover)
ISBN-10: 1-4048-2195-3 (hardcover)
ISBN-13: 978-1-4048-2201-6 (paperback)
ISBN-10: 1-4048-2201-1 (paperback)
1. Erosion—Juvenile literature. I. Harrad, Matthew, ill. II.
Title. III. Series.
QE571.K558 2007
551.3'02—dc22   2006008319

Printed in the United States of America in North Mankato, Minnesota.
082014
008384R

Table of Contents

The Forces of Change

A brick building on a street corner is crumbling away. A deep crack runs through the parking lot. Higher up, a building teeters on a muddy hillside.

What caused the changes in the brick building, the parking lot, and the hillside? It was erosion. Erosion is the wearing away and reshaping of the land. The forces of erosion have been changing Earth's surface for millions of years.

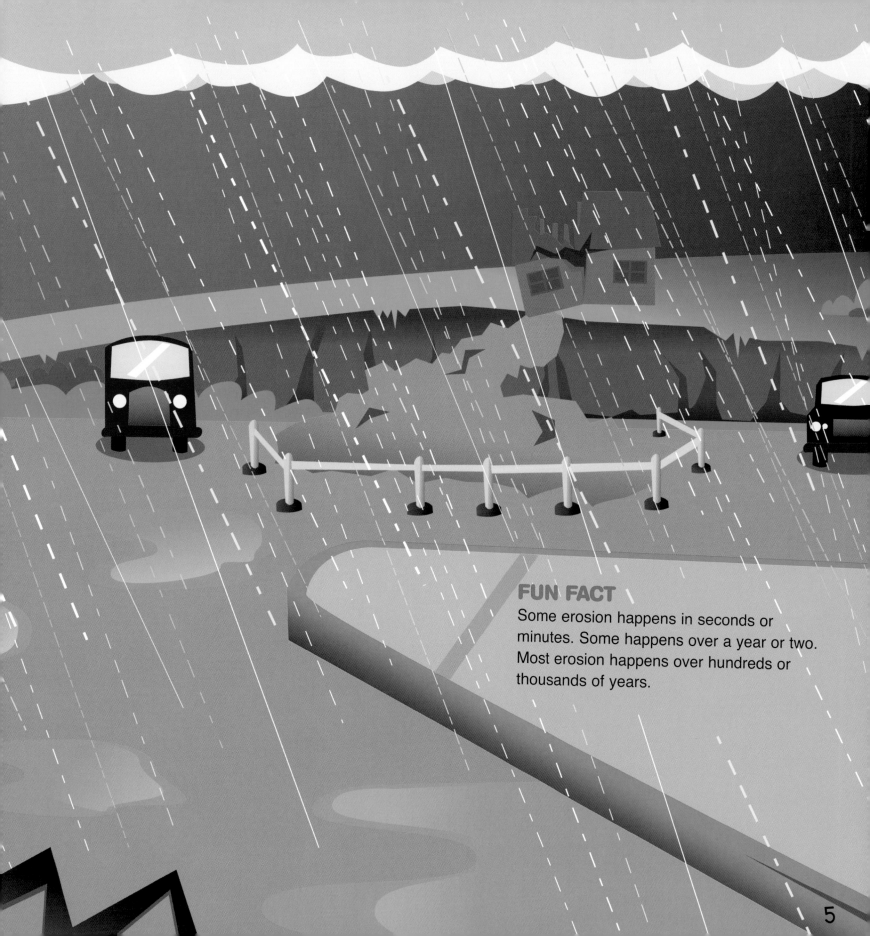

FUN FACT

Some erosion happens in seconds or minutes. Some happens over a year or two. Most erosion happens over hundreds or thousands of years.

Dripping Rain

Erosion can begin with a few drops of rain. The raindrops form a stream of water. The rainwater stream picks up dirt along the way. The stream gets bigger and races down the street. Be careful, because sometimes water pools in the street. Sometimes the water grows deep quickly.

FUN FACT
Sudden, heavy rain causes flash floods. Fast-flowing rainwater can be powerful enough to move houses and cars.

Roaring Rivers

The stream from the street joins with other streams and pours into lakes and rivers. The water picks up rocks along the way. The rocks grind along the bottom of the riverbed. The flowing water also washes dirt from the riverbanks. In these ways, rivers can cut deep gaps through the landscape.

Rivers flow to the oceans and leave behind a lot of dirt. The dirt is made of sand, pebbles, soil, and rocks. It is full of good nutrients for growing plants.

FUN FACT

Waterfalls can form when water flows over soft rock. The waterfall seems to move backward as it erodes, or cuts away, the rocks behind it.

Crashing Waves

Strong ocean waves crash against the shore. Ocean water slowly erodes soft rock and breaks chunks off the bottoms of the cliffs. The waves throw the loose material back against the shore. Eventually, the cliffs break apart from the crashing.

The power of waves can erode about 3 feet (1 meter) from a cliff each year. But what waves take away, they can wash back somewhere else. The eroded pieces from rocky cliffs can become a sandy beach not far away.

FUN FACT
A tsunami (pronounced soo-NAH-mee) is a huge wave that can cause lots of erosion in one giant sweep.

Frozen Erosion

Water seeps into cracks between rocks. After the water freezes, the ice expands, or gets bigger. The force of the ice is so strong that it can break up the rocks. Ice can crack streets and sidewalks in the same way.

Glaciers are like giant rivers of ice. They form in high places and move downhill. As they travel, they pick up dirt and rocks. They are like bulldozers that carve away mountains. Glaciers leave deep valleys. As the ice melts, the loose dirt and rocks get dumped on the land.

FUN FACT
The fastest glacier known to scientists moves 131 feet (40 m) per day, but most glaciers move only a few feet per day. Glaciers carve out U-shaped valleys. Rivers create V-shaped valleys.

13

Carving Caves

Drip, drip, drip. Raindrops slip past tree roots and erode away soft rocks underground. Little cracks get bigger. Over a long period of time, raindrops can carve out large underground caves.

Underground, raindrops pick up chemicals from the soil and soft rocks. They become a mix of rainwater, acids, and minerals. Inside the caves, the chemicals create new rocks. The dripping drops make stalactites on the ceiling and stalagmites on the cave floor.

Whipping Wind

Wind is the other force of erosion, and wind batters everything in its path. Wind can wear away buildings and carve away stone. Wind also has help to do its work. Sand carried by the wind rubs against objects that the wind hits.

Wind can form sand dunes and make sharp rocks smooth. Wind can also lift up soil and carry it away. Like rain, wind has a bigger effect on land with few plants.

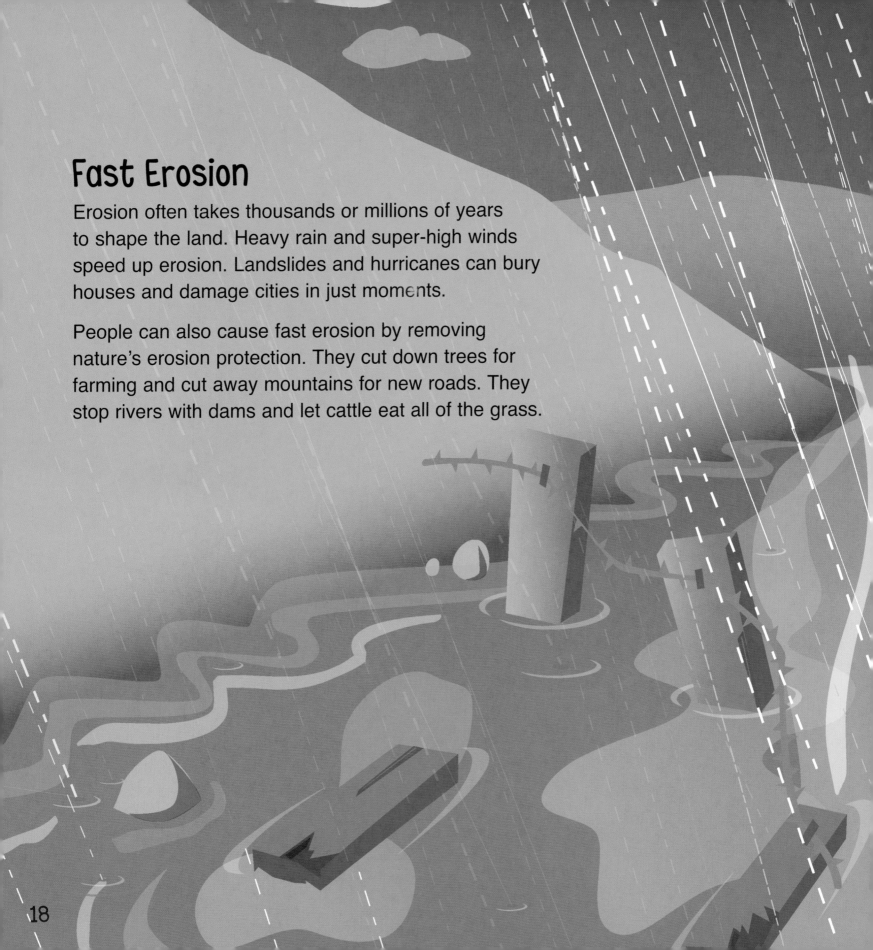

Fast Erosion

Erosion often takes thousands or millions of years to shape the land. Heavy rain and super-high winds speed up erosion. Landslides and hurricanes can bury houses and damage cities in just moments.

People can also cause fast erosion by removing nature's erosion protection. They cut down trees for farming and cut away mountains for new roads. They stop rivers with dams and let cattle eat all of the grass.

NOT-SO-FUN FACT
In the 1930s, U.S. farmers lost tons of soil to wind. There were no plants to keep the soil from blowing away. The sky turned black as winds carried away bits of soil. The eroded farmland was called the Dust Bowl.

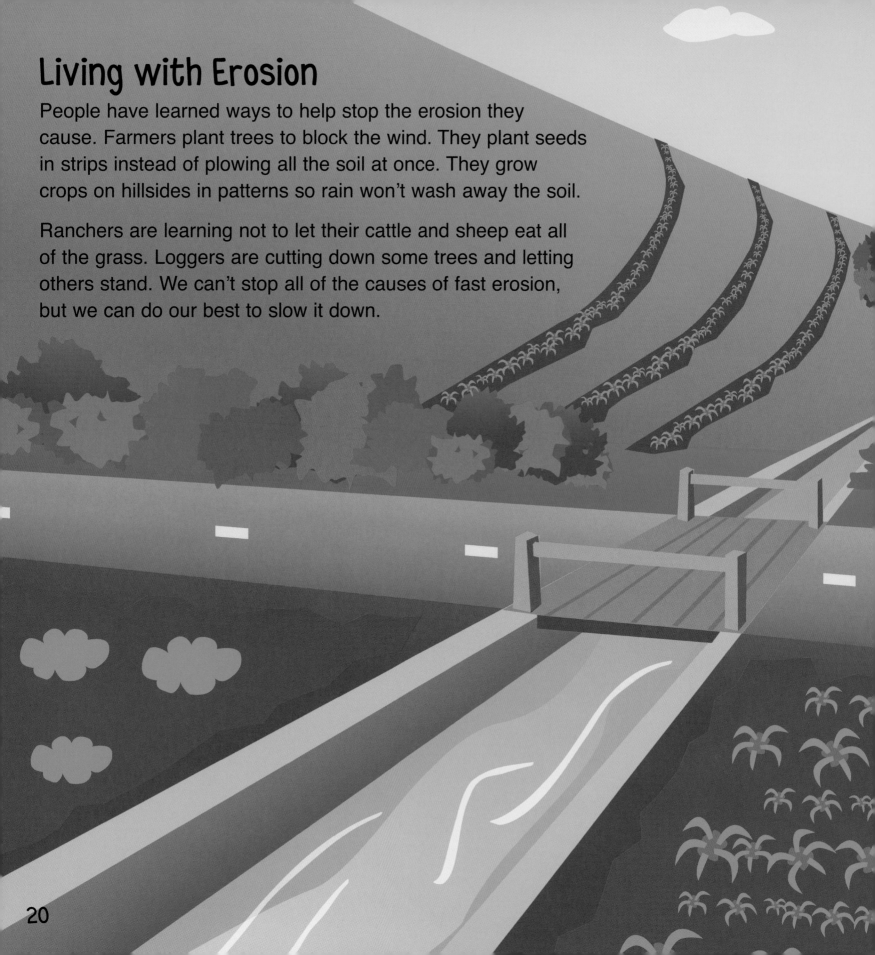

Living with Erosion

People have learned ways to help stop the erosion they cause. Farmers plant trees to block the wind. They plant seeds in strips instead of plowing all the soil at once. They grow crops on hillsides in patterns so rain won't wash away the soil.

Ranchers are learning not to let their cattle and sheep eat all of the grass. Loggers are cutting down some trees and letting others stand. We can't stop all of the causes of fast erosion, but we can do our best to slow it down.

FUN FACT

Drains and sewers near buildings and roads let rainwater run away quickly and safely. Without them, there would be more erosion of gardens, yards, parks, and playing fields.

21

Make a River

What you need:
- a strong piece of cardboard
- a bucket of sand
- a block of wood or a box
- a full pitcher of water

What you do:
1. Work outside! Wet the sand in the bucket.
2. Put the sand on the cardboard. Make hills and valleys so it looks like a real landscape.
3. Put the block or box under one end of the cardboard so it tilts slightly.
4. Slowly pour the pitcher of water on the high end of the sandy landscape.
5. Watch how the water travels and cuts the quickest path to the bottom. Notice how water carries sand with it.
6. Make a new landscape and try tilting the landscape to the right or left. See if anything different happens.

What do you think will happen to your sandy landscape if you pour more slowly or more quickly?

What do you think will happen if you pour water on dirt, rock, or concrete?

Erosion Extras

Bioerosion

Worms, snakes, and moles cause erosion by digging in the soil. Tree roots can also break up the ground. These types of erosion are called bioerosion.

Pollution and Erosion

Erosion on farmland can have a bad effect on the soil. If chemical fertilizers and pesticides are used, the leftovers can run into streams, ponds, and lakes. The water can become polluted.

Acid Rain

Humans are the main cause of acid rain. Chemicals from factories and car fumes go into the air and later come back in rain, sleet, snow, and even fog. This polluted water is called acid rain. It erodes rock and concrete, kills plants, and poisons fish in lakes and streams.

Rivers of Ice

The world's glaciers take up about 5.8 million square miles (14.8 million square km), an area as big as South America.

Glossary

dune—a hill of sand piled up by the wind

landscape—the form of the land in a particular area

passages—chambers or tunnels inside a cave

stalactites—growths that hang from the ceiling of a cave and were formed by dripping water

stalagmites—growths that stand on the floor of a cave and were formed by drips of water from above

To Learn More

More Books to Read

Colson, Mary. *Crumbling Earth.* Chicago: Raintree, 2004.

Downs, Sandra. *Shaping the Earth—Erosion.* Brookfield, Conn.: Twenty-First Century Books, 2000.

Olien, Rebecca. *Erosion.* Mankato, Minn.: Bridgestone Books, 2002.

On the Web

FactHound offers a safe, fun way to find Web sites related to topics in this book. All of the sites on FactHound have been researched by our staff.

1. Visit *www.facthound.com*
2. Type in this special code: 1404821953
3. Click on the FETCH IT button.

Your trusty FactHound will fetch the best sites for you!

Index

Look for other books in the Amazing Science series:

Air: Outside, Inside, and All Around
Composting: Nature's Recyclers
Dirt: The Scoop on Soil
Electricity: Bulbs, Batteries, and Sparks
Energy: Heat, Light, and Fuel
Light: Shadows, Mirrors, and Rainbows
Magnets: Pulling Together, Pushing Apart
Magnification: A Closer Look
Matter: See It, Touch It, Smell It
Motion: Push and Pull, Fast and Slow
Rocks: Hard, Soft, Smooth and Rough
Science Measurements:
   How Heavy? How Long? How Hot?
Science Safety: Being Careful
Science Tools:
   Using Machines and Instruments
Sound: Loud, Soft, High, and Low
Temperature: Heating Up and Cooling Down
Water: Up, Down, and All Around